Maa; You scold, but you love

Mrigendra Bharti

Published by Sellbrochure Entertainment Vymish, 2024.

MAA; YOU SCOLD, BUT YOU LOVE

First edition. June 3, 2024.

ISBN: 979-8227911582

Written by Mrigendra Bharti.

Dedication

In the stillness of dawn and the whispers of dusk, this book stands as a monument to the unparalleled love and unwavering strength of mothers. To the architects of our earliest memories, the guardians of our deepest secrets, and the champions of our wildest dreams, this dedication flows like a river of gratitude, boundless and eternal.

For every sleepless night spent cradling us in your arms, for every tear wiped away with gentle hands, for every sacrifice made in the name of our happiness, this book serves as a testament to your immeasurable love and boundless grace.

Through the highs and lows, the triumphs and tribulations, you have been our guiding light, our unwavering support, our source of infinite wisdom. Your nurturing embrace has been a sanctuary in times of turmoil, your soothing voice a melody in the cacophony of life.

With each word penned in these pages, we strive to capture the essence of your indomitable spirit and immortalize the legacy of your love. From the tender moments shared in laughter and joy to the profound lessons learned in times of adversity, your presence has shaped us into the individuals we are today.

From the depths of our souls to the expanse of the universe, this dedication echoes the sentiment of countless hearts: you are cherished, you are revered, you are loved beyond measure. Your love is the foundation upon which we build our lives, the beacon that guides us through the darkest nights.

This book is dedicated to you, dear mothers, with deepest gratitude and boundless admiration. May its pages serve as a tribute to your immeasurable impact and a reminder of the eternal bond that unites us.

To the timeless essence of maternal love,
In the tapestry of life's grand design,
This book is a humble offering,
To the architects of our dreams,
The guardians of our hearts,
The light that guides our way,
To mothers everywhere,
Whose love knows no bounds,
Whose strength knows no limit,
Whose grace knows no end.
With each word penned,
With each line woven,
We honor your legacy,
And celebrate your spirit,
In every heartbeat,
In every breath,
In every word,
You are cherished,
You are revered,
You are loved.
This book is dedicated to you,
With deepest gratitude and boundless admiration.
Dedication:
To the timeless essence of maternal love,
In the tapestry of life's grand design,
This book is a humble offering,
To the architects of our dreams,
The guardians of our hearts,
The light that guides our way,
To mothers everywhere,
Whose love knows no bounds,

Whose strength knows no limit,
Whose grace knows no end.
With each word penned,
With each line woven,
We honor your legacy,
And celebrate your spirit,
In every heartbeat,
In every breath,
In every word,
You are cherished,
You are revered,
You are loved.
This book is dedicated to you,
With deepest gratitude and boundless admiration.

In the stillness of dawn and the whispers of dusk, this book stands as a monument to the unparalleled love and unwavering strength of mothers. To the architects of our earliest memories, the guardians of our deepest secrets, and the champions of our wildest dreams, this dedication flows like a river of gratitude, boundless and eternal.

For every sleepless night spent cradling us in your arms, for every tear wiped away with gentle hands, for every sacrifice made in the name of our happiness, this book serves as a testament to your immeasurable love and boundless grace.

Through the highs and lows, the triumphs and tribulations, you have been our guiding light, our unwavering support, our source of infinite wisdom. Your nurturing embrace has been a sanctuary in times of turmoil, your soothing voice a melody in the cacophony of life.

With each word penned in these pages, we strive to capture the essence of your indomitable spirit and immortalize the legacy of your love. From the tender moments shared in laughter and joy to the profound lessons learned in times of adversity, your presence has shaped us into the individuals we are today.

From the depths of our souls to the expanse of the universe, this dedication echoes the sentiment of countless hearts: you are cherished, you are revered, you are loved beyond measure. Your love is the foundation upon which we build our lives, the beacon that guides us through the darkest nights.

This book is dedicated to you, dear mothers, with deepest gratitude and boundless admiration. May its pages serve as a tribute to your immeasurable impact and a reminder of the eternal bond that unites us.

With love and appreciation,

Mrigendra Bharti

Preface:

In the journey of life, there exists a guiding force, an everlasting source of love and strength—our mothers. They are the unsung heroes, whose nurturing embrace shapes our dreams and anchors our souls. "Mumma: You Scold, but You Love" is a collection of heartfelt poems dedicated to the eternal bond between a mother and her child.

Through the verses of this book, we explore the myriad emotions experienced in the presence of a mother—the warmth of her love, the wisdom of her words, and the comfort of her embrace. Each poem is a tribute to the selfless sacrifices made by mothers, and a celebration of the profound impact they have on our lives. As you embark on this poetic journey, may you find solace in the universal language of love and gratitude. May these words serve as a reminder of the invaluable role played by mothers in shaping our destinies. And may you, dear reader, cherish the precious moments spent in the company of your own beloved mother.

With love and reverence,

Mrigendra Bharti

Foreword:

In the tender tapestry of life, few relationships weave threads as enduring as that between a mother and her child. It is a bond forged in the fires of love, nurtured by sacrifice, and strengthened by unwavering devotion. "Mumma: You Scold, but You Love" is a testament to the profoundness of this bond—a collection of verses that pay homage to the guiding light that is a mother's love.

As I reflect on the pages of this book, I am reminded of the countless moments shared with my own mother—her gentle caress, her reassuring words, and her boundless affection. Each poem within these covers encapsulates the essence of maternal love, capturing its essence in words that resonate with the heart.

Through laughter and tears, triumphs and trials, our mothers stand by us with unwavering support. They are our pillars of strength, our voices of reason, and our wellsprings of love. In "Mumma: You Scold, but You Love," we honor the countless sacrifices made by mothers, and celebrate the infinite depths of their love.

To the readers embarking on this poetic journey, may you find solace in the verses that follow. May they serve as a reminder of the boundless love that surrounds us, and the irreplaceable role played by mothers in shaping our lives.

With gratitude and admiration,

Mrigendra Bharti

Prologue:

In the realm of human emotions, there exists a sentiment so profound, so enduring, that it defies the boundaries of time and space. It is the love of a mother—a force that transcends words, yet finds expression in the simplest of gestures. "Mumma: You Scold, but You Love" is a tapestry woven from the threads of this timeless love—a collection of poems that seeks to capture the essence of the maternal bond.

As we journey through the pages of this book, we embark on a voyage of remembrance and reflection. Each poem serves as a mirror, reflecting the myriad facets of maternal love—the tenderness of a mother's touch, the strength of her resolve, and the wisdom of her counsel. Through verse, we explore the depths of emotion that define the relationship between a mother and her child.

But beyond the words themselves lies a deeper truth—a truth that speaks to the universal nature of maternal love. Whether through laughter or tears, joy or sorrow, mothers remain steadfast in their devotion, their love an unwavering beacon in the stormy seas of life. In "Mumma: You Scold, but You Love," we pay homage to this enduring love, and celebrate the indelible mark it leaves on our hearts.

To the readers who embark on this poetic journey, may you find solace in the verses that follow. May they serve as a reminder of the immeasurable value of a mother's love, and the countless blessings it brings into our lives.

Acknowledgment:

In the creation of any work, there are countless individuals whose contributions, support, and inspiration deserve recognition. "Mumma: You Scold, but You Love" is no exception, and it is with heartfelt gratitude that I acknowledge those who have played a pivotal role in bringing this collection to fruition.

First and foremost, I extend my deepest appreciation to my own mother, whose love and guidance have shaped me into the person I am today. Your unwavering support and boundless affection serve as the foundation upon which this book stands.

I am also grateful to my family and friends, whose encouragement and belief in my abilities have sustained me throughout this journey. Your faith in me has been a constant source of strength and inspiration.

To the readers who embark on this poetic voyage, I extend my sincere thanks for your interest and support. It is my hope that the verses within these pages resonate with you, and serve as a tribute to the universal language of maternal love.

Last but not least, I would like to express my gratitude to the countless poets and writers whose works have inspired me over the years. Your words have ignited my imagination and kindled the flames of creativity within me.

In closing, I offer my deepest thanks to all who have contributed to the creation of "Mumma: You Scold, but You Love." Your love, encouragement, and support have made this journey possible, and for that, I am eternally grateful.

Introduction:

Welcome to "Mumma: You Scold, but You Love," a collection of poems dedicated to the extraordinary bond between a mother and her child. Within these pages, we embark on a journey of reflection, gratitude, and celebration as we explore the profound impact of maternal love.

The relationship between a mother and her child is one of the most enduring and powerful connections in the human experience. It is a bond forged in the crucible of love, strengthened by sacrifice, and illuminated by unconditional devotion. In this collection, we delve into the depths of this timeless bond, seeking to capture the essence of maternal love in verse.

Each poem within these covers is a testament to the myriad emotions evoked by the presence of a mother—the warmth of her embrace, the wisdom of her words, and the constancy of her support. From moments of joy and laughter to times of sorrow and strife, mothers stand as beacons of strength and compassion, guiding us through life's ever-changing landscape.

As we journey through the verses of "Mumma: You Scold, but You Love," may we find solace in the universal language of love and gratitude. May these poems serve as a tribute to the immeasurable impact of maternal love, and a reminder of the blessings that mothers bestow upon us each and every day.

So let us turn the page and embark on this poetic odyssey, honoring the mothers who have shaped our lives and celebrating the boundless depth of their love.

With heartfelt appreciation,

Mrigendra Bharti

Author Biography

Mrigendra Bharti, born on June 29, 2004, in South Delhi, India, is a multifaceted individual recognized as the owner of Mrigendra Bharti Group InfoTech India Co. Pvt Ltd. Beyond his entrepreneurial endeavors, he is a distinguished music producer, director, and a budding writer.

Embarking on his professional journey at a young age, Mrigendra Bharti's visionary leadership has led to the establishment of several successful ventures, including Croma Music Series Entertainment, Sellbrochure, Fauget Innovative, and more.

What sets Mrigendra apart is his early initiation into the world of business. His foray into the unknown realms of entrepreneurship began during his 10th-grade years, where he delved into the music industry. This initial venture laid the foundation for subsequent achievements, showcasing his dedication and resilience.

Having honed his skills in music, Mrigendra Bharti not only demonstrated significant growth in his craft but also expanded his professional network. His passion extends beyond music, encompassing app and website development, as well as graphic design.

Fueled by his creative aspirations, Mrigendra established the Mrigendra Bharti Group, a company specializing in website and app development. Currently, he collaborates with a dedicated team, collectively working on ambitious projects that promise innovation and excellence.

Mrigendra's journey serves as an inspiration, particularly for today's students, highlighting the potential of youthful determination and the ability to transform innovative ideas into successful businesses. As he continues to make strides in various domains, Mrigendra Bharti remains a dynamic force, contributing vibrancy to the realms of business, music, and technology.

Poem 1

In the quiet of night, when all is still,
Your love surrounds me, a comforting thrill.
With tender care, you soothe my fears,
Mumma dear, your presence endears.
Your gentle touch, a beacon bright,
Guiding me through the darkest night.
In your embrace, I find solace deep,
Mumma, your love, a treasure to keep.

Poem 2

In your eyes, I see a world of dreams,
A love so pure, it forever gleams.
With every step, you light my way,
Mumma dear, you guide me day by day.
Your gentle hands, a haven sweet,
In your embrace, all troubles fleet.
With whispered words, you calm my fears,
Mumma dear, you dry my tears.
In your smile, I find my cheer,
A beacon bright, dispelling every fear.
With boundless love, you fill my soul,
Mumma dear, you make me whole.

Poem 3

In the quiet of night, I hear your voice,
A melody sweet, my heart's rejoice.
Your words of wisdom, like a guiding light,
Mumma dear, you make everything right.
Through stormy seas and darkest night,
Your love shines bright, a guiding light.
With every hug, with every kiss,
Mumma dear, you fill me with bliss.
In your arms, I find my peace,
A sanctuary where worries cease.
With every heartbeat, with every breath,
Mumma dear, you conquer death.

Poem 4

In your laughter, I find my joy,
A melody that no time can destroy.
With every smile, you light my way,
Mumma dear, you brighten my day.
In your patience, I find my strength,
A pillar of support, of boundless length.
With every challenge, with every test,
Mumma dear, you bring out my best.
In your forgiveness, I find my grace,
A second chance, a warm embrace.
With every mistake, with every fall,
Mumma dear, you forgive them all.

Poem 5

In your kitchen, I find my home,
A place of comfort, where memories roam.
With every dish, with every meal,
Mumma dear, you make it all real.
In your stories, I find my truth,
A wisdom passed down from age to youth.
With every tale, with every rhyme,
Mumma dear, you stand the test of time.
In your hands, I find my care,
A touch so gentle, beyond compare.
With every gesture, with every touch,
Mumma dear, you give so much.

Poem 6

In your silence, I find my peace,
A calmness that will never cease.
With every quiet moment shared,
Mumma dear, I know you've cared.
In your prayers, I find my hope,
A faith that helps me to cope.
With every word, with every plea,
Mumma dear, you pray for me.
In your dreams, I find my aim,
A vision that ignites my flame.
With every wish, with every goal,
Mumma dear, you make me whole.

Poem 7

In your eyes, I see my reflection,
A glimpse of love, a deep connection.
With every glance, with every stare,
Mumma dear, you're always there.
In your hands, I find my security,
A touch that fills me with purity.
With every grasp, with every hold,
Mumma dear, you make me bold.
In your heart, I find my home,
A place of love, where I never roam.
With every beat, with every pulse,
Mumma dear, you are my eternal source.

Poem 8

Amidst the chaos, you're my calm,
In your embrace, I find my balm.
With every storm, with every squall,
Mumma dear, you stand tall.
In your laughter, I find my song,
A melody that keeps me strong.
With every giggle, with every chuckle,
Mumma dear, you make life sparkle.

Poem 9

Beneath the stars, I hear your call,
A whisper soft, yet strong and tall.
With every night, with every moon,
Mumma dear, you're my cocoon.
In the sunrise, I see your grace,
A radiant glow upon your face.
With every dawn, with every light,
Mumma dear, you shine so bright.

Poem 10

In the garden of life, you're my bloom,
A flower that dispels all gloom.
With every petal, with every hue,
Mumma dear, you renew.
In the symphony of existence, you're my note,
A melody that keeps me afloat.
With every chord, with every tune,
Mumma dear, you make me swoon.

Poem 11

In the tapestry of time, you're my thread,
A constant presence, by my side you tread.
With every stitch, with every weave,
Mumma dear, you never leave.
In the gallery of memories, you're my art,
A masterpiece that touches my heart.
With every stroke, with every hue,
Mumma dear, you paint my view.

Poem 12

In the vast ocean, you're my shore,
A steady anchor forevermore.
With every wave, with every tide,
Mumma dear, you're by my side.
In the forest of dreams, you're my tree,
A sheltering canopy, strong and free.
With every leaf, with every branch,
Mumma dear, you enhance.

Poem 13

In the melody of life, you're my song,
A tune that keeps me moving along.
With every note, with every rhyme,
Mumma dear, you're my rhythm divine.
In the canvas of dreams, you're my color,
A vibrant hue that makes life fuller.
With every stroke, with every shade,
Mumma dear, you never fade.

Poem 14

In the silence of night, you're my calm,
A soothing presence, a healing balm.
With every whisper, with every hush,
Mumma dear, you quell the rush.
In the garden of love, you're my bloom,
A fragrant flower, banishing gloom.
With every petal, with every scent,
Mumma dear, you're heaven-sent.

Poem 15

In the vast expanse of sky, you're my star,
A guiding light from afar.
With every twinkle, with every gleam,
Mumma dear, you're my cherished dream.
In the symphony of nature, you're my melody,
A harmonious tune that sets me free.
With every note, with every chord,
Mumma dear, you're my sweet reward.

Poem 16

In the dance of time, you're my beat,
A rhythm that makes my life complete.
With every step, with every sway,
Mumma dear, you light my way.
In the book of life, you're my story,
A tale of love, grace, and glory.
With every chapter, with every page,
Mumma dear, you're my guiding sage.

Poem 17

In the garden of my heart, you're my flower,
Blooming with love, hour by hour.
With every petal, with every scent,
Mumma dear, your love is heaven-sent.
In the symphony of emotions, you're my melody,
Harmonizing life's discord with glee.
With every note, with every tune,
Mumma dear, you make my world attune.

Poem 18

In life's journey, you're my companion,
Walking together, in every condition.
At every step, in every path,
Dear Mumma, you're my strength.
In the gallery of memories, you're my example,
Filling every moment with happiness ample.
Every moment, every memory, in your embrace,
Dear Mumma, you're my companion in this space.

Poem 19

In the melody of existence, you're my tune,
A harmonious rhythm under the moon.
With every beat, with every note,
Mumma dear, in your love, I float.
In the canvas of dreams, you're my art,
A masterpiece etched within my heart.
With every stroke, with every hue,
Mumma dear, you make my dreams come true.

Poem 20

Amidst the symphony of life, you're my melody,
A soothing tune that sets my soul free.
With every chord, with every refrain,
Mumma dear, you ease every pain.
In the tapestry of dreams, you're my thread,
Stitching moments of joy in life's spread.
With every stitch, with every weave,
Mumma dear, you're the love I receive.

Poem 21

In the garden of my heart, you're my bloom,
Radiant and beautiful, dispelling gloom.
With every petal, with every scent,
Mumma dear, your love is heaven-sent.
In the symphony of emotions, you're my song,
A melody that keeps me moving along.
With every note, with every tune,
Mumma dear, you brighten my monsoon.

Poem 22

In the book of my life, you're the chapter,
Guiding me through every disaster.
With every page, with every line,
Mumma dear, your love divine.
In the canvas of my dreams, you're the paint,
Adding colors to life, without restraint.
With every stroke, with every shade,
Mumma dear, in your love, I'm swayed.

Poem 23

In the symphony of my journey, you're the melody,
A harmonious tune that fills me with glee.
With every note, with every beat,
Mumma dear, you make my life complete.
In the tapestry of my memories, you're the thread,
Binding moments together, as we tread.
With every stitch, with every seam,
Mumma dear, you're my guiding beam.

Poem 24

In the whispers of the wind, you're my calm,
A gentle breeze, like a soothing balm.
With every rustle, with every sway,
Mumma dear, you light up my day.
In the depths of my heart, you're my anchor,
Keeping me steady, amidst the anger.
With every pulse, with every beat,
Mumma dear, you make my life sweet.

Poem 25

In the tapestry of my life, you're the color,
Brightening my days, like no other.
With every hue, with every shade,
Mumma dear, in your love, I'm swayed.
In the symphony of my soul, you're the melody,
A harmonious tune that sets me free.
With every note, with every chord,
Mumma dear, you are adored.

Poem 26

In the garden of my heart, you're the blossom,
Radiant and beautiful, amidst life's awesome.
With every petal, with every scent,
Mumma dear, your love is heaven-sent.
In the rhythm of my days, you're the beat,
Guiding my steps, keeping me fleet.
With every pulse, with every thump,
Mumma dear, you're my eternal hump.

Poem 27

In the embrace of my dreams, you're the whisper,
Guiding me through every twilight, every glimmer.
With every whisper, with every sigh,
Mumma dear, you're my endless sky.

Poem 28

In the tapestry of life, you're my thread,
Stitching moments of love, wherever we tread.
With every stitch, with every line,
Mumma dear, your love forever shines.
In the symphony of my soul, you're the song,
A melody that keeps me strong.
With every note, with every chord,
Mumma dear, you're my compass, my lord.

Poem 29

In the garden of my soul, you're the bloom,
A flower of love, dispelling gloom.
With every petal, with every scent,
Mumma dear, your love is heaven-sent.
In the melody of my life, you're the tune,
A song of joy, under the moon.
With every verse, with every rhyme,
Mumma dear, you make every moment sublime.

Poem 30

In the canvas of my existence, you're the paint,
Adding colors of love, without restraint.
With every stroke, with every hue,
Mumma dear, my gratitude to you.
In the symphony of my journey, you're the melody,
Guiding me through life's vast sea.
With every note, with every beat,
Mumma dear, you make my life complete.

Poem 31

In the sanctuary of my heart, you're the light,
Guiding me through the darkest night.
With every glow, with every gleam,
Mumma dear, you're my eternal dream.
In the mosaic of my memories, you're the piece,
A cherished treasure that will never cease.
With every fragment, with every part,
Mumma dear, you're the essence of my heart.

Poem 32

In the symphony of my life, you're the melody,
A sweet refrain that brings harmony.
With every note, with every chord,
Mumma dear, you are adored.
In the tapestry of my days, you're the thread,
Binding moments together, where love is spread.
With every stitch, with every seam,
Mumma dear, you're my guiding beam.

Poem 33

In the garden of my soul, you're the sun,
Radiating warmth, where love is spun.
With every ray, with every shine,
Mumma dear, your love is divine.
In the melody of my heart, you're the song,
A sweet refrain that keeps me strong.
With every verse, with every rhyme,
Mumma dear, you're my guiding sign.

Poem 34

In the tapestry of my life, you're the color,
Vibrant and bright, like no other.
With every hue, with every shade,
Mumma dear, in your love, I'm swayed.
In the rhythm of my days, you're the beat,
Guiding my steps with every feat.
With every pulse, with every thump,
Mumma dear, you're my eternal hump.

Poem 35

In the constellation of my dreams, you're the star,
Shining brightly, from afar.
With every twinkle, with every gleam,
Mumma dear, you're my guiding beam.
In the melody of my thoughts, you're the rhyme,
A soothing rhythm, in the chime.
With every lyric, with every verse,
Mumma dear, you're my universe.
In the tapestry of my emotions, you're the thread,
Binding me close, where love is spread.
With every stitch, with every seam,
Mumma dear, you're my eternal dream.

Poem 36

In the garden of my spirit, you're the bloom,
Radiant and lovely, chasing away gloom.
With every blossom, with every scent,
Mumma dear, your love is heaven-sent.
In the rhythm of my existence, you're the beat,
Guiding my steps, making life sweet.
With every pulse, with every thud,
Mumma dear, you're my source of good.

Poem 37

In the symphony of my life, you're the conductor,
Guiding me through each note, each juncture.
With every wave of your baton,
Mumma dear, my spirit you spawn.
In the tapestry of my days, you're the weaver,
Crafting moments of love, of fervor.
With every thread, with every strand,
Mumma dear, you hold my hand.

Poem 38

In the sanctuary of my soul, you're the light,
Guiding me through the darkest night.
With every flicker, with every glow,
Mumma dear, your love I'll always know.
In the melody of my heart, you're the tune,
A sweet refrain that banishes gloom.
With every rhythm, with every beat,
Mumma dear, you make my life complete.

Poem 39

In the gallery of my memories, you're the masterpiece,
A work of art that will never cease.
With every stroke, with every line,
Mumma dear, your love forever shines.
In the melody of my dreams, you're the song,
A harmonious tune that keeps me strong.
With every note, with every chord,
Mumma dear, you're my guiding sword.

Poem 40

In the garden of my heart, you're the blossom,
Radiant and vibrant, banishing any gloom.
With every petal, with every hue,
Mumma dear, your love shines true.
In the symphony of my life, you're the melody,
A sweet refrain that sets me free.
With every note, with every tune,
Mumma dear, you make my world attune.
In the tapestry of my memories, you're the thread,
Binding moments together, where love is spread.
With every stitch, with every seam,
Mumma dear, you're my guiding beam.

Poem 41

In the gentle embrace of dawn's first light,
Your love shines through, pure and bright.
With every smile, with every hug,
Mumma dear, you're my eternal tug.
In the whispers of the wind, I hear your voice,
Guiding me through life's every choice.
With every word, with every prayer,
Mumma dear, you're always there.
In the depths of my soul, your love resides,
A comforting presence that never hides.
With every beat, with every breath,
Mumma dear, you conquer death.
In the tapestry of my life, you're the thread,
Binding moments together, where love is spread.
With every stitch, with every seam,
Mumma dear, you're my guiding beam.

Poem 42

In the garden of my heart, you're the bloom,
Radiant and vibrant, chasing away gloom.
With every petal, with every hue,
Mumma dear, your love shines true.
In the melody of my days, you're the song,
A sweet refrain that keeps me strong.
With every verse, with every rhyme,
Mumma dear, you make every moment sublime.
In the canvas of my dreams, you're the paint,
Adding colors of love, without restraint.
With every stroke, with every shade,
Mumma dear, in your love, I'm swayed.

Poem 43

In the journey of my life, you're the guide,
Walking beside me, side by side.
With every step, with every stride,
Mumma dear, you're my constant pride.
In the gallery of memories, you're the art,
Painting my life with love from the start.
With every brushstroke, with every scene,
Mumma dear, you're my eternal queen.

Poem 44

In the symphony of my soul, you're the melody,
A harmonious tune that sets me free.
With every note, with every chord,
Mumma dear, you are adored.
In the tapestry of my memories, you're the thread,
Binding moments together, where love is spread.
With every stitch, with every seam,
Mumma dear, you're my guiding beam.

Poem 45

Amidst the pages of my life, you're the story,
A narrative of love, in all its glory.
With every chapter, with every line,
Mumma dear, your love forever shines.
In the tapestry of my existence, you're the thread,
Weaving moments of joy, where love is spread.
With every strand, with every weave,
Mumma dear, you're the love I believe.

Poem 46

In the sanctuary of my heart, you're the calm,
A soothing presence like a healing balm.
With every breath, with every sigh,
Mumma dear, you're my lullaby.
In the symphony of my life, you're the melody,
A sweet refrain that brings harmony.
With every rhythm, with every beat,
Mumma dear, you make my life complete.

Poem 47

In the tapestry of my days,
you're the sunshine,
Radiant and warm,
in every line.
With every dawn,
with every ray,
Mumma dear,
you light up my way.
In the melody of my dreams,
you're the star,
Guiding me through life,
Near and far.
With every twinkle,
With every gleam,
Mumma dear,
You're my eternal dream.

Poem 48

Within the tapestry of my being,
you're the thread,
Stitching moments of love,
where paths we tread.
With every stitch,
with every line,
Mumma dear,
Your love forever shines.
In the melody of my soul,
You're the song,
A sweet refrain that keeps me strong.
With every verse,
with every rhyme,
Mumma dear,
You make my spirit chime.

Poem 49

In the whispers of the night, you're the star,
Shining bright, no matter how far.
With every twinkle, with every gleam,
Mumma dear, you're the light of my dream.
In the depths of my heart, you're the ocean,
Endless and vast, in loving devotion.
With every wave, with every tide,
Mumma dear, you're my eternal guide.
In the tapestry of my dreams, you're the weaver,
Crafting stories of love, where hearts never sever.
With every thread, with every stitch,
Mumma dear, you're the love I'll never ditch.
In the melody of my life, you're the note,
A symphony of love, that forever floats.
With every tune, with every chord,
Mumma dear, you're my compass, my lord.
In the garden of my soul, you're the bloom,
Radiant and vibrant, chasing away gloom.
With every petal, with every scent,
Mumma dear, your love is heaven-sent.

Poem 50

In the silence of the night, you're the whisper,
A gentle voice that brings calmness hither.
With every murmur, with every sigh,
Mumma dear, you're the reason why.
In the tapestry of my dreams, you're the color,
Painting life's canvas with hues much fuller.
With every stroke, with every hue,
Mumma dear, you make dreams come true.
In the melody of my heart, you're the rhythm,
A steady beat that banishes any whim.
With every thump, with every beat,
Mumma dear, my love for you is complete.
In the sanctuary of my soul, you're the light,
Guiding me through the darkest night.
With every flicker, with every glow,
Mumma dear, your love continues to flow.

Poem 51

In the symphony of my life, you're the conductor,
Guiding me through each note, each juncture.
With every wave of your baton,
Mumma dear, my spirit you spawn.
In the tapestry of my days, you're the weaver,
Crafting moments of love, of fervor.
With every thread, with every strand,
Mumma dear, you hold my hand.
In the gallery of my memories, you're the art,
A masterpiece that touches my heart.
With every stroke, with every hue,
Mumma dear, your love shines through.

Conclusion

In the tapestry of life, amidst every rhyme,
Mumma dear, you've stood the test of time.
With every verse, with every line,
Your love, dear Mumma, forever shines.
As we close this chapter, let us not forget,
The love and warmth that weaves our net.
In every word, in every plea,
Mumma dear, you're our eternal glee.
So let these poems serve as a token,
Of the love that's never broken.
In every stanza, in every verse,
Your love, dear Mumma, we rehearse.
With heartfelt thanks and gratitude,
We end this book with certitude.
Mumma dear, you're our guiding light,
Forever shining, forever bright.

Thanks Note

I extend my heartfelt thanks to you, dear readers, for embarking on this poetic journey with me through the pages of "Mumma: You Scold, but You Love."

Your willingness to immerse yourselves in these verses is truly humbling, and I am grateful for your time and attention. It is your support and appreciation that breathe life into these poems, giving them meaning and purpose beyond the words on the page.

Your presence as readers enriches this book and fills its pages with warmth and connection. Thank you for allowing me to share my thoughts and emotions with you through the medium of poetry.

May these poems resonate with you, touch your hearts, and remind you of the immeasurable love and bond between a mother and her child.

With deep gratitude,

Mrigendra Bharti

About the Author

Mrigendra Bharti, born on June 29, 2004, in South Delhi, India, is a multifaceted individual recognized as the owner of Mrigendra Bharti Group InfoTech India Co. Pvt Ltd. Beyond his entrepreneurial endeavors, he is a distinguished music producer, director, and a budding writer.

Embarking on his professional journey at a young age, Mrigendra Bharti's visionary leadership has led to the establishment of several successful ventures, including Croma Music Series Entertainment, Sellbrochure, Fauget Innovative, and more.

What sets Mrigendra apart is his early initiation into the world of business. His foray into the unknown realms of entrepreneurship began during his 10th-grade years, where he delved into the music industry. This initial venture laid the foundation for subsequent achievements, showcasing his dedication and resilience.

Having honed his skills in music, Mrigendra Bharti not only demonstrated significant growth in his craft but also expanded his professional network. His passion extends beyond music, encompassing app and website development, as well as graphic design.

Fueled by his creative aspirations, Mrigendra established the Mrigendra Bharti Group, a company specializing in website and app development. Currently, he collaborates with a dedicated team, collectively working on ambitious projects that promise innovation and excellence.

Mrigendra's journey serves as an inspiration, particularly for today's students, highlighting the potential of youthful determination and the ability to transform innovative ideas into successful businesses. As he continues to make strides in various domains, Mrigendra Bharti remains a dynamic force, contributing vibrancy to the realms of business, music, and technology.

Read more at https://www.imwriter-mrigendra.rf.gd.